Living a
Victorious Life
From the Bottom to the Top

Bruce Atchison

TEACH Services, Inc.
PUBLISHING
www.TEACHServices.com • (800) 367-1844

Copyright © 2022 Bruce Atchison
Copyright © 2022 TEACH Services, Inc.
ISBN-13: 978-1-4796-1471-4 (Paperback)
ISBN-13: 978-1-4796-1472-1 (ePub)
ISBN-13: 978-1-4796-1473-8 (Mass Market)
Library of Congress Control Number: 2022904851

All scripture in this book is taken from the King James Version.

Published by

TEACH Services, Inc.
P U B L I S H I N G
www.TEACHServices.com • (800) 367-1844

Table of Contents

Foreword

by Mr. Ron Clark, educator, missionary,
church leader, and best friend

A re you satisfied with your life as it is? If so, this book is not for you. Are you serious about overcoming addictions, bad habits, or chronic choices? Then you will be encouraged and equipped as you read this short, but powerfully practical guide. It is the story of the life of one person who found the path out and has made a map for fellow-travelers to follow!

The following pages are the fruit of over seventy years of life experience, twenty-eight of which were focused on work with drug and alcohol prevention for teens in public and church schools. What you are about to read is not only the story of one man's life, but also the solid, tried, and true steps that lead to victorious living. For this reason, the author lays out this map for you in reference form. That is, in addition to the story that punctuates the principles that the author shares, you will also receive your equipment along with practical application sheets. This is not theory; it is life experience! You have now entered the story that can be *your* story, and you have now embarked on a journey that holds a bright future for those who will follow the map.

Introduction

Dear reader, I would like to introduce myself to you first before we delve into my new book, *Living a Victorious Life from the Bottom to the Top*, for I have been at life's bottom, as I will fully develop in the chapters to follow.

Currently, I am seventy-four years young, but my first book compelled me to do a sequel to the subject of facing life's problems. So, why am I writing this book? I am writing it because the subject is very timely for many people who have suffered from failures and depression, who feel worthless, who are unliked by their peers, or who are just plain disadvantaged from life's earliest days.

My personal life had many of these same issues, which, later on, included smoking and drinking, among other things. These took their toll on me. I failed at basically everything I did academically. If it were not for being drafted into the military at age nineteen, I would have been totally lost in what to do in this world. After my discharge from the United States Air Force in 1970, I went to junior college but only to fail again in the first year of school. Three D's did not put me on a track to success. By God's grace, I kept at it and changed my major. A year later, I transferred to Cal State University at Northridge, California. From then on, I spent all my available time studying so that I ended up finishing with a bachelor of science in recreation administration with a C+ average. Later on, at the age of thirty-three, I went to Cal State, Chico, to complete my master's degree. By that time, I had grown from being a failure in life to being set up for success. But did the higher degree mean that I would not suffer failure again? It did not!

Looking back, with three strikes against me—the least likely to succeed in high school, unliked by girls, and totally unable to succeed academically—I could have retreated permanently from the batter's box of life. But Mom and Dad would not have their son's life be a failure. Their prayers and God's leading got me through. So, I invite you now to enjoy reading my life story and be blessed, for, with God's help, you too can succeed, make others proud of you, and put a smile on God's face.

My encouragement to you is to "go for it" under the power of Jesus' Holy Spirit, who can help you to be all that you were created to be.

Sincerely yours,
Bruce

Chapter 1

My Life Testimony

D ear reader of this book, I am now seventy-four years young, and practicing what I preach, I can say that living a healthy life has extended my life so I can lecture, write, and help others.

As you have seen, my dear friend, Ron Clark, wrote the foreword for me. I had the privilege of working with Ron for six of the twenty-eight years that I served as a field representative for Community Crusade Against Drugs (CCAD). I also have spent the last two years lecturing adults on how to break bad habits.

When in the classroom, talking with teens aged thirteen to eighteen, my goal was to educate them on prevention, but it was also to help them make life choices to avoid alcohol, smoking, and drugs. I quickly found out that many of my students smoked, drank, and used various drugs. When I learned this, I changed tactics to include my life story, describing how I was a smoker, a drinker, and a marijuana (MJ) user. "Yes, my young friends," I would say, "I used these substances, but, if I had to do it over again, I would have lived my life differently."

I like to believe that my testimony made a difference for the thousands of teens I spoke to. Based on that belief, in writing the outline for this book, I was impressed to go back into my past life and review how I got to be a smoker, drinker, and MJ user. Was it by accident or by choice, or was I set up by early life situations out of my control?

As I write about my early years, I do so with deep emotions. For you see, I was brought up in a Christian family. Neither Mom nor Dad ever drank or smoked. So, I cannot blame them for passing on bad genes or for giving me a bad example when I was a teenager.

So, what went wrong? How did I get to be a smoker and drinker in my teen years? Well, here I go to help you understand me better; and, later in this book, you will see my life open up like a beautiful flower, showing how God helped me change the direction of my life and overcome my bad habits.

❝ *In looking back, I realize that my life goal of becoming a professional baseball pitcher was a long shot.*

Friends, I still have my report cards from grades one through nine that remind me of that discouraging period, as I struggled with a learning disorder. Back in 1947, when I was born, and as I grew up, such disorders were not so well understood. So, Mom and Dad might have missed a better way to deal with their son.

To add to this, when I was twelve, I came down with mononucleosis, also called the "kissing disease." My white blood cell count was so high that I was at first diagnosed as having leukemia. The sickness caused me to lose a full year of my life. With concerns about my passing on the "kissing disease" to others, the teacher put me in the back of the room to keep from infecting the other students. It might be something like the concerns about COVID-19 in 2020. And what were the results? My brain function was damaged, and I felt like a zero. Also, being ostracized made me feel unwelcomed by the other students.

Failing academically, the only positive for me in school was baseball. You see, I could throw many types of pitches to get a batter out. I worked at this by the hour in my neighborhood and backyard. Six feet, four inches tall, I was also a good basketball player, so I thought the sport would be the only way I could achieve success in life. To realize this dream, I took myself out of church school and enrolled in a very large public high school.

Thus, at age seventeen, I left the religion and church of my parents and, in so doing, broke their hearts. My next step was to try out for the baseball team. The school had 4,000 students, and my graduating class was 1,500 strong. In looking back, I realize that my life goal of becoming a professional baseball pitcher was a long shot. I made the varsity team, but I failed as a pitcher and was sent to the junior varsity team. Sorry to say, I was not used for one minute the whole baseball season. This destroyed me! Now I was a failure again.

So, between my junior and senior years of high school, I took up smoking cigars. To fit in with the wrong group, I also started going to bars when I was eighteen because I looked like an adult. When I was nineteen, I was to graduate. So, I took the United States Air Force test and failed as well. My life story was one failure after another. With no military available at this time, I joined the United States Forest Service to be a fire fighter. I worked there for nine months and loved it. At the end of this work period, I received a "love letter" from—you guessed it—the United States Army draft board. They said: We want you to go and fight for us during the Vietnam War. No way did I want to go and fight and get killed fighting for something that I did not agree with. So, what to do? Well, back to the United States Air Force recruiter.

I asked him, "Can I beat this draft order?"

"Yes, you can."

Praise the Lord! I thought. So I retook the entrance test, and this time I passed it. What a blessing this became! Now I could use my brain instead of killing others.

I was sworn in on the spot into the Air Force reserves, and, a few months later, I was called to active duty. When I went to Amarillo, Texas, for basic training, I was still a smoker. When my team messed up, we all had to forfeit smoking privileges. So, I decided to quit, and I did so. However, my drinking only picked up because my friends, like most military men, drank. Sometimes I drank like a fish and was ready to fight everyone who came into my presence. Overall, my years in the U.S. Air Force were tops. I was a jet engine mechanic, and I advanced to the level of a three-stripe sergeant. This put me on flight duty, and I even went to Greenland for a two-month stay. After that, I was stationed at the Edwards Air Force Base in California.

From my military stint, which was mostly a success, I went on, at twenty-three years of age, to start college. I went to a junior college, and my first year I got three D's. What was I to do now? I was highly motivated to succeed in school, but my lack of a solid background in math, science, and English really hurt me now. I took inventory of what I was able to do. I could throw a baseball and shoot a basketball with the best of them. So, I chose a career track in recreation administration. At Cal State, Northridge, California, I finally started to be a success in school because my brain could understand business, management, and leadership classes. I even was selected as a class president. What a change for me! Me, a leader if you will. After getting a bachelor of science in college, I moved to Alaska and became an administrator with the parks and recreation department in Anchorage. I worked there for almost three years. Afterward, I became athletic director for the Boy's Club of Alaska. To relieve my stress from this high-pressure job, I again drank like a fish and was very close to becoming an alcoholic.

Wouldn't you know it, I lost my dream job to another person and had become a failure again. But now I was determined to go back to school again. So, off I went to Cal State, Chico, in Northern California. My life goal was to get an MA in Recreation Administration and Park Planning. Little did I know that this school was voted by *Playboy* magazine as the most partying school in America that year. This did not do well with me since I was still smoking MJ and drinking alcohol. MJ almost made me lose my desire to finish school as it did for others in my class. If it had not been for living with my mom and dad in Paradise, California, I would have fallen by the wayside as well. MJ is the lazy person's drug. It makes you forget about your life goals and just chill out.

But God had a plan to help me overcome this life problem. Mom and Dad had daily devotion time with God, and they asked me to join them. Sometimes I responded with a straight "no" and sometimes "maybe later." In addition to drawing me toward being a Christian, I was introduced to a couple who loved Jesus. We enjoyed talking about the Lord, and I was soon coming to church. This led to my dating a Christian lady and having Bible studies with the pastor. Soon God helped me overcome MJ and drinking alcohol—cold turkey.

Chapter 2

Testimony Continued

S o, following my early life experience, I was now finishing my master's degree. Yet, I still struggled against all odds. My project paper was turned down. Heartbroken, I gave up since I am not a writer. I failed freshman English twice, and the third time I got a C. I certainly was not on the dean's list!

My reader friends, from the many failures in my early life, I now entered a period where some successes came. Yes, there were many self-imposed errors, but now there were also victories.

How sweet it is to go from a "Z" life plan to an "A" life plan! At the age of thirty-five, I now entered post-seminary training, as a layperson, in a Bible school that was in Chicago under the leadership of Mark Finley. This nine-month school-training period, which was my first formal training on the subject of the Bible, led me to complete the class curriculum and earn a Bible instructor certificate. What I was to do with that new training was a subject of much prayer. At that time, I received a call from Pennsylvania from John Hoch, the local Review and Herald district leader, to come and take over the fledgling drug education program called the *Listen* Community Crusade Against Drugs (CCAD). Friends, I had to really scratch my head and even pull out some hair, for I could not understand why God would train me to be a Bible worker and then move me to a totally different career area.

So, I prayed on this and felt that Providence was moving me to accept this call. Next, I drove to Wilkes-Barre, Pennsylvania in the month of October 1983. With my new leader, Mr. John Hoch, I started my new duties. These duties included fund-raising, school lecturing, and working with the communities CCAD's goal to stem the spread of junior and senior high school drug, alcohol, and smoking usage.

Would you believe that my only training for this calling was that I smoked cigarettes from the ages of seventeen to nineteen, drank alcohol from age eighteen on, and later smoked MJ in Alaska with my druggy brother and later in the most partying college in America?

> **❝***How sweet it is to go from a "Z" life plan to an "A" life plan!*

The type of training for my new calling was truly not the kind one would get in college. God has a sense of humor. That He put me in this position as a businessperson and educator with little training was a miracle in the making.

I started out working in a section of Scranton, Pennsylvania. My face-to-face duties of fundraising was a stretch for me, and I was not well blessed at first. It took about three months to go to every business in Scranton and finally raise the needed money to fund seven schools, including one Catholic school. When I visited with a business owner and CEO, I told my story about my use of drugs. Soon I was asked to talk to the teens. The program expanded very rapidly. Soon I was working all over northeast Pennsylvania. Over thirty schools used my services, and, over the

next twenty-eight years, I lectured to thousands and thousands of teens. In addition, I talked to thousands of business owners and CEOs to raise the needed funds.

While in the classroom, as a drug and alcohol prevention educator, the first thing the teens would ask me was, "Did you do them yourself?"

"Well, yes," I would tell them, "but, if I had to do it again, I would not live life the same way. This usage of drugs is not the best way to go, my young friends. So, do as I now say and not as I once did." To get this point across, I would go on to describe my drug addicted brother's experience. He started using MJ when he was fifteen with our friends on the block where we lived in Los Angeles, in the San Fernando Valley. When I told them how my brother Norm now had multiple addictions that included cigarettes, MJ, alcohol, and harder drugs, it got their attention. The use of drugs is truly a chain. Norm worked at all the major Hollywood studios for the better part of thirty-four years. He told me how drugs were a part of the culture of the actors and actresses.

I learned by trial and error what was the best way to reach the teens' growing minds. My experience and training for teaching these young people led me to watch many videos, read books, and prepare lectures on what I heard from the health teachers and others. After doing a few assemblies of a whole grade of 100 young people or more, I transitioned to teaching only a classroom at a time. It was a much easier way to manage the teens. I brought into the classroom real lungs, livers, and large pictures of what happens when you smoke, drink, or use drugs. I even used the blackboard to draw out the cycle of addiction. The health teachers loved me because I "told it like it is" when they were not able to address it in the way I did to educate the teens to quit using drugs or to never start in the first place.

I was blessed to be able to do this mission work for God for twenty-eight years. In 2011, *Listen* magazine was pulled from production and my career in drug usage prevention was over. With *Winner* magazine having been pulled in 2009, all the tools to help educate teens were gone. Sadly, I had to leave my calling. What I took from these twenty-eight years was my experience with many professional organizations—such as the Lions Club, the Kiwanis Club, and the Rotary Club—I talked with to raise money to fund schools. The training I received by working with businesses and adults gave me a life tool for educating adults. So, now, at the age of sixty-four, I was too young to retire. What would I do next in life?

As adults, we all are struggling with addictions of one sort or another. So, I felt that I could now be used by God to help adults or perhaps teens again, but what exactly would I do? I started to research all self-supporting organizations within the Seventh-day Adventist Church and sent resumes to many of them.

I got a call from Gayle Clark, CEO of Miracle Meadows School in West Virginia, a Christian boarding school for at-risk kids from ages seven to eighteen. I went down to visit the school and later accepted the call to work there. For almost three years, I worked there as their fundraising director and safety officer, with any other administrative duties they needed. I retired at the age of sixty-seven because the work burned me out fast. I had learned much from this tour of duty.

Now I was retired, but God was not done with me yet. So my next calling was to write a manual of nine lectures on how to break bad habits. For almost a whole year, I researched the human brain about how living an intemperate life affects what we do and the decisions we make. When I was done, I lectured to churches in West Virginia for almost two years. Then, I started my own online Christian bookstore.

In chapter 1 of the manual, I shared how God's Holy Spirit-directed power would give any person the victory if they fully surrendered their lives to God. I included a step-by-step process to help each student understand how to live a victorious life and overcome any addiction or life problem. I could see that God wanted me to continue to help adults, but I still felt a little void in my life not helping teens with their problems. However, this might come back to reality with the advent of a new career—writing Christian books and lecturing wherever God directs me to go.

Chapter 3

Spirit Victory Through God's Power

We cannot overcome addictions through a life change alone. We must have God's grace and power working in our hearts. Alcoholics Anonymous (AA) says, in step one of their twelve-step program: "We admitted we were powerless over alcohol—that our lives had become unmanageable." While God gave me total victory over alcohol and MJ, both at once, and did so cold-turkey, I had to now accept God fully and work my program daily—even hourly—to maintain the victory that God wanted me to have. Why? The habit that I had was hard-wired in my brain, which would need to be rewired. The 100 billion neurons of the brain are pathways connected by synapses, which pass electrical charges at a very high rate of speed and create something that can be thought of as either a rivet or a deeper groove in the brain. These pathways, which are made over years of a chemical usage, must be reconnected in a different way as new habits are formed. These changes take time. The brain keeps the old channels for many years, and a person can easily slip back into the old habits. This is why we must now tap into God's living power 24-7 and stay connected to live a victorious new life. The good news is that, over the years of God's working in us, we are blessed to be new creatures, as the apostle Paul says, forgetting the past and moving on (Philippians 3:13, 14).

But the bottom line is that we must sense our utter helplessness, as the apostle Paul did in Romans 7:24, 25. When we sense our nothingness and are willing to see our smallness, in other words, when we surrender to His power and tell Him to manage our heart, then we are blessed for victory.

In our world now, Jesus is readily accepted as a Savior for our sins but not so readily accepted as Lord over our lives. Both are

> **❝When we surrender to His power and tell Him to manage our heart, then we are blessed for victory.**

necessary for complete victory. Our will surrendered and our minds and bodies yielded to God, the Holy Spirit can come in and grant us His grace, which equals His power to work in us. God's word written in His holy Bible is the key. When we subscribe to "every word that proceedeth out of the mouth of God" (Matthew 4:4), we are on the road to victory over sin, our bad habits, and whatever else confronts us spiritually.

The Bible says that the Holy Spirit helps us obey God's Word (1 Peter 1:22). In verse 23, it says that we are reborn, or born again, into God's image by the "word of God." In 2 Peter 1:21, it says that prophecy, God's teaching, came by "holy men of God" as they spoke and wrote scripture by "the Holy Ghost," the third member of the Godhead.

This is the gospel, God's good news, for remember that, by ourselves, we cannot break any bad habit 100%. Even the strongest among us—say the 10% of people with a strong will—cannot do it on their own. A complete heart and life change demands that we have God in us, the hope of glory.

John 14:26 describes the ministry of the Holy Spirit, who is the Comforter that we all need. "He shall teach you all things, and bring all things to your remembrance." In the process of our victory, it is positively "one day at a time." We must work daily at this process of victory. Never forget that we have an enemy, Satan, who is trying to undo all that God does for us. Not for a millisecond can we forget this and try to do this on our own. For, you see, to rewrite a brain pathway needs at least three weeks before a new pathway is developed and the simplest change in a habit can occur. In many cases, it takes months and years to have a solid new pathway develop. I well remember when I was in the classroom, teaching the teens not to smoke, drink, or do drugs. Each time

I told them not to do drugs, this truth etched my brain pathway more solidly so that I would never again desire to go back to my prior lifestyle.

To summarize, what Jesus is looking for in you and me is a heart emptied of self-importance. Then the Holy Spirit, through God's Word and prayer, will lead us to hunger and thirst for God's righteousness and right doing. With the power of Christ in us, we are then victorious in Jesus. Can you join with me in saying "amen and amen again" and "praise the Lord" for doing in us what we can never do for ourselves?

Now to help your victory be more solid, please fill out the worksheet, "Spirit Victory Through God's Power."

Spirit Victory Through God's Power

1. I can do all things through Christ that strengthens me.
   Y __ N __

2. If I am on the wrong path of life, through humility as a child, I can get back on the correct path.   Y __ N __

3. I can do things myself.   Y __ N __

4. By giving praises to God I can be victorious.   Y __ N __

5. I am willing to be taught by God.   Y __ N __

6. I must have daily communion with Christ.   Y __ N __

7. What will happen to me if I refuse to listen to the prompting of the Holy Spirit?

   _____

   _____

8. If I refuse to be baptized by fire and to experience a change of my old life, what will my spiritual life be like?

   _____

   _____

9. Through trials, God purifies me.   Y __ N __

10. My daily cry must be for more of Him.   Y __ N __

11. For daily victory I must live up to all the light that I have been given.   Y __ N __

12. What will happen if I fail to live up to the light I know?

   _____

13. We need to grow daily.   Y __ N __

14. Victory is assured if we look to the cross and see what our sins cost Jesus and then refuse to hurt Him again.   Y __ N __

15. With open communion with Jesus, sin will become hateful to us.   Y __ N __

16. Daily small victories lead to larger ones.   Y __ N __

17. My faith grows stronger and stronger as I gain daily victories over sin and the devil.   Y __ N __

Chapter 4

Our Choices

As we learn in the first step of Alcoholics Anonymous, the first principle of overcoming is to admit that we have a problem. Now, as we have seen, our problem—whether it is self or something else—requires that we make positive choices to break free. David wrote: "Our soul is escaped as a bird out of the snare of the fowlers: the snare is broken, and we are escaped. Our help is in the name of the LORD, who made heaven and earth" (Psalm 124:7, 8).

The third step of Alcoholics Anonymous is: "Made a decision to turn our will and our lives over to the care of God ...." In the chapter, "The Sinners Need of Christ," in the little book by Ellen G. White, *Steps to Christ*, she says, "Education, culture, the exercise of the will, human effort, all have their proper sphere, but here they are powerless. They may produce an outward correction of behavior, but they cannot change the heart; they cannot purify the springs of life. There must be a power working from within, a new life from above, before men can be changed from sin [which is our human problem] to holiness. That power is Christ. His grace alone can quicken the lifeless faculties of the soul, and attract it to God, to holiness" (p. 18). In John 3:3, Jesus said to you and me, "Except a man be born again, he cannot see the kingdom of God." With God's power now working in us, we have some skeletons in our closet we need to deal with.

I well remember after I got out of the United States Air Force in 1970, at the tender age of twenty-three, that the Holy Spirit was working on my heart. John 16:8 says that the Spirit will convict us "of sin, and of righteousness, and of judgment."

And, oh boy, what the Holy Spirit can do for us when we have a tender, open heart! Guilt and our sin separate us from God (see Isaiah 59:2). So we need to deal with it, period!—not run away as Adam and Eve did in the garden when they "hid themselves from God" (Genesis 3:8).

> **66** *And, oh boy, what the Holy Spirit can do for us when we have a tender, open heart!*

Friends, Jesus says, "Come unto me." We have a loving Savior who, with open arms, invites us to come to Him, and the really good news, as found in John 6:37, is "him that cometh to me I will in no wise cast out." I have done that and found myself welcomed home from a wild life of alcohol, MJ, and women. But I certainly needed purity in my life.

So now that I was married for the second time, God clearly spoke to me about tools I had stolen from the U.S. Air Force. How I was to deal with this fact sent shock waves through my mind. Had I not come to start to trust in God? Well, yes! But I was a new babe in Christ, yet with fear. I got the toolbox together and decided to go to the local Air Force recruiter.

"Sir," I said to him, "you will not believe this, but, since I have become a Christian, I am under the conviction that I must return these tools to you."

Do you have any questions? Has anyone else done likewise?

Friends, I had no fear doing this. So, when I left his office "guilt free," my new life had one less entanglement in which Satan could trap me. With a clear conscience, I have now told many people over the years about my life changing choice.

Yes, it was tough, but, oh how good it felt to have God with me as well as the courage to do what is right! Righteousness is God's goal for you and me. Right doing is critical for us. Our daily choices either bring us to God or they drive us away from Him. My daily choice from 1983 until the present has been to put God first. Daily I study my Bible, daily I pray for God's guidance, and daily I try to help others.

Friends, we must work out our salvation by faith in God's Word as led by the Holy Spirit—not with fear but by God's love being manifested in us. Good works are the fruit of the Holy Spirit found in us. The revealed fruits of the Spirit are found in Galatians 5:22, 23.

So, make the best choices daily. Always put God first to be your number one friend. Now please fill out the worksheet, "Our Choices."

Our Choices

1. Do our choices impact our character as a person? Y __ N __.
   Explain.

   _____

   _____

2. Bad choices cause us consequences! Name them.

   _____

   _____

3. What good choice did Daniel make? (See Daniel 1:8.)

   _____

   _____

4. Do you wish to choose to make a lifestyle change? Y __ N __.
   Which one?

   _____

   _____

5. What benefit will you gain from this choice?

   _____

   _____

6. What risks do you run if you do not make this positive choice
   now?

   _____

   _____

7. Good information is needed to decide on a lifestyle change. What information do you need to read or hear to make this new lifestyle change?

_____

_____

Let me encourage you to follow through on your decision.

8. Having identified your need of a lifestyle change, what goals can you make now to see your lifestyle a success?

Short-term changes, such as _____

_____ Long-term changes, such as _____

_____

9. How do you plan to follow this daily goal?

_____

_____

10. Was this a good choice to make now?   Y __ N __

11. What can you do differently to make sure you keep to your decision for success?

_____

_____

12. Remember that Daniel "purposed in his heart [or mind] that he would not defile himself" (Daniel 1:8). The word "purposed" can also be worded as "determined." The power of the will, rightly set, is like a rudder on a ship, steering through choppy waters.

_____

_____

"Discipline is the bridge between goals
and accomplishment."
—Jim Rohn

Chapter 5

Overcoming Temptation

My friends, we ended chapter 4 with the importance of putting God first in our lives. With God first and the teachings of His Word in me, I have a moral compass to help me make the best and safest choices.

So, as we enter chapter 5, "Overcoming Temptation," we must realize that an "adversary" has existed since the dawn of earth's history, beginning after Adam and Eve fell to Satan's temptations. In Genesis 3:1, a serpent, which was Satan, tempted Eve by causing her to doubt God's word. She knew (verse 3) that God had said not to eat or touch it—period—that is, the fruit "of the tree of the knowledge of good and evil" (Genesis 2:17).

To that point, why was a test tree in the garden in the first place? Good question, wouldn't you say? To get the answer, we must go to the book of Revelation. Revelation 12:7 says, "There was war in heaven." A battle took place between God's angels and Satan's angels. Scripture says, in verses 8 and 9, that Satan lost the battle, and "he was cast out into the earth, and his angels were with him." So, we can clearly see that the devil that was in heaven is the same devil that tempted Eve in the garden. Further, in verse 12, we read, "Woe to the inhabitants of the earth."

The serpent has "great wrath" for all of the population of planet earth. We now get the picture. To the extent that God allows him, Satan has had the ability to tempt, destroy, and cause trouble for all of earth's population. In 2 Peter 5:8, it says, "The devil ... walketh about seeking whom he may" destroy—which is the condition that can be clearly seen in our present world.

Now, back to answering why there was a test tree. Could it be a test of loyalty? You see, God created our world perfect. Genesis 1:31 describes man as "very good." Humankind was given a free will to be able to choose which one he would serve, for the God of love created us in His image like Himself, and love is only love when freely given and accepted.

So, would Adam and Eve obey the command to show their love and trust to God, or would they obey the serpent? A test tree in the garden would show the entire universe and the angels in heaven which way humankind chose to go and which master they would serve. Satan, who we know to be a conman, dressed himself as a beautiful talking snake, if you will. Genesis 3:6 says that the devil used sight, one of our senses, to get Eve. It says the fruit was "pleasant to the eyes." Eve reasoned, with her free will, that the fruit was "desired to make one wise." What a top temptation Satan used to deceive Eve! So, here is a question: If he could do that in a perfect world, nailing Eve, what can he do with us today in a fallen sinful world?

My dear friends, Satan uses the strongest temptation in the world to nail us at our weak points. In 1 John 2:15, God tells us to not do the things of the world, for if we "love the world, the love of the Father is not" in us. In verse 16 of the same chapter, John tells us how the old serpent goes out to get us, through—

1. "The lust of the flesh," which includes sex and any pleasure that is not God given,
2. "The lust of the eyes," which might include a big house, a fast car, a sexy woman or man, or other things we long after,
3. "The pride of life" that "is of the world." Proclaiming, "I am number one, the best of the best, look at me!"

To help you see this clearly, I have included the worksheet, "The Temptation Cycle."

The Temptation Cycle

1. At what point must you decide to ask for help from God while being tempted?

    A. Point of being tempted Y __ N __

    B. Before point of temptation Y __ N __

    C. While being tempted Y __ N __
    D. I can do this myself. Y __ N __

    (Is it a good or a bad choice to do this myself?)

    _____

2. My choice leads to either victory or defeat. Y __ N __

3. Am I drawn away by my desires? Y __ N __
   (To lust, appetite, worldly power, etc.)

    A. If I lust for these three areas, will I be enticed to sin?
       Y __ N __

    B. Once I sin, can I break free with God's help? Y __ N __

    C. If I stay lusting, I can lose it all! Y __ N __

4. James 4:7 says to submit to God. My daily choice is a must here. Y __ N __. Explain your answer.

    _____

    _____

    (I should submit to God hour by hour. Y __ N __)

5. Resisting Satan means letting God draw me to Him and making a decision to get His help. Prayerful Bible study is a must on a daily, moment by moment basis. Y __ N __

6. Once I let God draw me, I must avoid sinful areas! James 4:8 and 1 Peter 1:22 gives us good advice to be victorious. Read

and memorize these verses. We need to internalize God's Word and memorize it. His Word cleanses up my life.

_____

_____

7. Good habits are formed or evil habits by what? Hebrews 5:14 says "senses exercised," by "reason of use." "Use" means habitual use-repeated choices for good. By using God's Word, we can then make choices to discern good or evil. Am I drawn to God? Y __ N __. Am I drawn to evil? Y __ N __. 2 Peter 2:14.

_____

_____

8. We are tested/tried for what reasons? Malachi 3:2, 3.

_____

_____

9. We must also be prepared to resist for a period of time. Y __ N __ In Matthew 4:1–11, Jesus had to resist for a period of time. In Galatians 6:9, we learn that we must "not grow weary in good doing." Y __ N __

> "The higher the hill, the stronger the wind: so the loftier the life, the stronger the enemy's temptations." —John Wycliffe.

James 1:12 tells us that we all must endure temptation. All held hostage on planet earth by Satan must be tried like Adam and Eve were in the garden of Eden. Why is that? To show our love for Him—Jesus Christ. Verse 14 says, when a man "is tempted," he is "drawn away of his own lust, and enticed." Being drawn away from God, we sin against Him.

Now let's look at the Christian fish (ichthys) symbol below.

The Crossfire!

On a PERSONAL level
Loyal to God, faithful to Jesus

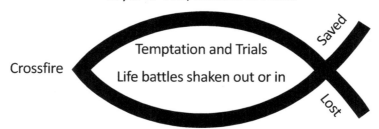

Rebels to God, Satan's Army
On a UNIVERSAL level!

While in Chicago studying with pastor Mark Finley, we had a Bible study student who could not give up smoking. So, we decided that he should come and stay with us at our living center. At the time, God impressed me to use the fish symbol and the Bible book of James to draw out what actually happens in the great controversy between Christ and Satan. So, when this young man saw the choices he had and the power of God to help him, he quit at once. His choices were:

   A. Ask for help in prayer and be drawn to God, or
   B. Let himself to be enticed and fall for Satan's temptation.

James 1:14 describes being drawn away from God's help. Friends, the devices Satan uses to destroy—the lust of the flesh and eyes and the pride of life—must be resisted and overcome. But how do we do that?

   1. First, go back and review "The Temptation Cycle" worksheet, filling it out if you have not already done so, and you will see some answers on how to resist and overcome.
   2. Then, review the fish symbol and put yourself and your tempted areas into the graphic.

3. To further answer your Holy Spirit revealed questions, the next chapter entitled, "What to Do When Tempted," will help you overcome the devil and his evil angels who spend all their time trying to tempt and destroy us twenty-four hours a day, seven days a week, 365 days out of the year.

Chapter 6

What to Do When Tempted

W hat should we do now that we are being tempted? Should we give up and just enjoy it? Should we let ourselves be injured? Should we fall into sin against God's laws of love, which is our moral protection? Or is there hope to avoid being tempted and not just survive but flourish in God's love as one of His sons and daughters?

Part A. What to Do When Tempted

A life story will help you now. When working on my master's degree at Chico State University in Chico, California, a professor led our Wednesday night social and Bible study. He taught us how to not only resist but to be forewarned before even being tempted. So how is that? Here are the steps:

1. Knowing that you are walking into potential trouble, always pray for God's protection and guidance that you may be led by the Holy Spirit and the holy angels. The apostle Paul says, in 1 Thessalonians 5:17, that we are to "pray without ceasing." In other words, we should always be in a spirit of prayer wherever we go.

2. We read in the book of Daniel (1:3, 4) that the king's army invaded Jerusalem and brought back choice young Hebrew men to Babylon. Daniel and his young friends, who were of royal seed, were marched as captives on a one-month trek to Babylon. As they travelled, they pondered what to expect when they arrived in Babylon. Once at the king's palace, they were to be given "of the king's meat, and of the wine which he drank" (Dan. 1:5), which would include unclean meats. The four Hebrew boys knew that unclean meats were not on the

diet given them by God and that they could not obey Him and partake of it. Also, because they were designated for service in the temple, they did not drink wine at all. They knew that drinking wine would affect their minds, causing them not to be sharp in school learning. So, what were they to do now under this major temptation? Should they be faithful to their God and His health laws, or should they succumb to taste and the lifestyle of the king? They could do but one thing. Daniel 1:8 says that he "purposed in his heart," that is, that he *determined*, to consume none of the king's meat or wine.

3. The Bible also teaches that we are to pray while under attack in any situation. An example would be, when we see a friend smoking, to throw up a quick prayer for help to resist the pressure to follow his example. In James 4:7 it says, "Resist the devil, and he will flee from you." Verse 8 says, "Draw nigh to God, and he will draw nigh to you." Please go back to the fish symbol and review it to see this choice in living color.

4. Also, we must be walking with Jesus 24/7/365 by talking to Him, studying His Word, and sharing it with others—in other words, following in the footsteps of Jesus. Jesus' personal example was a life of compassion, love, and healing of the lost.

Friends, if we follow Jesus' example, we will be protected while under the daily state of temptation. I personally have memorized Bible promises while under attack by Satan or his angels. I claim a Bible promise such as Philippians 4:13, "I can do all things through Christ which strengtheneth me." I know I cannot resist temptation under my own power, but, with Christ living in me and as led by the Holy Spirit, I can resist Satan's advances. We must always remember that Satan's only goal, as found in 1 Peter 5:8, is "seeking whom he may devour."

We read in Genesis 3:1–3 how Adam and Eve fell under temptation. In Genesis 2:17, God had warned Adam that, if he should disobey God's law of love, he would "surely die." In Genesis 3:4, the tempter countered God's warning saying, "Ye shall not surely die." Adam's sinful choice in disobeying God put planet earth into Satan's hands, and for the last six-thousand years Satan's only goal has been to cause as many humans as he can to sin against God so that they will be destroyed as were those who sinned before the Flood. Genesis 6:5 says of mankind at this time "that every imagination of the thoughts of his heart was only evil continually."

Friends, we must be on guard 24/7 all the days of our lives.

Before we move on, please fill out the three pages of the work-sheet, "What to Do When Tempted."

What to Do When Tempted

1. While Daniel was tempted, what did he do? (Daniel 1:8).

   _____

   _____

2. What did Joseph do when tempted? (Genesis 39:9).

   _____

   _____

3. What does James 1:19 tell me I must do?

   _____

   _____

   A. How often?

   _____

   B. Put what you must do in your own words.

   _____

4. What does James 4:8 tell me to do?

   _____

5. What did Peter do? (Matthew 26:33–35).

   _____

   This led to his downfall (see verse 58).
   Is it a good choice to sit with the rabble rousers? Y __ N __
   To prevent this downfall, what should Peter have done before
   he went into the palace area?

   _____

   _____

6. The apostle John made good choices. What are some examples? (John 18:15, 16).

   _____

   _____

7. When tempted to do evil, how are we to overcome? (Romans 12:20, 21).

   _____

   _____

8. Romans 6:16 says we are servants to whom we obey from the heart, whether we obey—
   A. Satan or
   B. God by obedience unto righteousness.

9. Jesus says He could do nothing on His own. What about us?

   _____

   _____

10. Jesus' own example is worth looking at in depth. In Matthew 4:3, Satan appealed to Jesus to cause a doubt in His mind—"If thou be the son of God ..." Y __ N __

11. In verse 4, what was Jesus' answer?

    _____

    _____

12. Satan did not give up. Disguised as an angel of light, he returned and said, "If thou be the son of God" (verse 6). What was Jesus' answer?

    _____

    _____

13. The devil now promises to give Jesus all He wanted, including a short-cut from the cross (verse 8) "If [a word expressive of conditionality] thou wilt fall down and worship me" (verse 9). Question: Was it in Satan's power to give Jesus all these things he promised? Y __ N __. Explain your answer.

_____

_____

14. Lastly, what was Jesus' answer (verse 10)?

_____

_____

Friends, Satan does not give up. This situation in the wilderness is proof. Our only hope in defending ourselves is to put on the whole armor of God and have God's Word engrafted in our minds. We must live by, "It is written"!

Part B. God's Promises

Jesus said in Matthew 7:7—

A. "Ask, and it shall be given you,"
B. "Seek, and ye shall find,"
C. "Knock, and it shall be opened unto you."

Friends, we must believe God's Word. We must only hang our hats for any security we have on God's promises. His Word is solid gold, for, in 2 Peter 1:4, His precious promises state that we will "be partakers of the divine nature, having escaped the corruption that is in the world through lust."

This is talking about Satan's three-part method to destroy us. Again, as found in 1 John 2:18, his method has to do with the lust of the flesh, the lust of the eyes, and the pride of life.

Our only safety is in believing God's Word.

In Jesus' story of the paralytic, at the pool of Bethesda, the poor, suffering people were helpless. So, where was the paralytic to put his hope? In someone to get him into the water first, or in something else? Jesus said, basically, in John 5:6—What do you want me to do? Or, more precisely—

1. "Wilt thou be made whole?"
2. The man responded: "Sir, I have no man to get me into the water."
3. Jesus said (and here is the power of His word), "Rise, take up thy bed, and walk."
4. So, the man arose, and he was made whole.

In a favorite book of mine, Ellen G. White says, "He *willed* to walk, and he did walk. He acted on the word of Christ, and God gave the power. He was made whole" (*Steps to Christ*, p. 50). She says further, "I believe it; it *is* so, not because I feel it, but because God has promised" (*Steps to Christ*, p. 51).

The power of God's Word requires belief. If you believe and act according to God's Word, He will help you. God's promises are fulfilled on condition that we pray according to God's will.

And those promises are also found in *Steps to Christ,* on page 51—
He promises to "cleanse us from sin, to make us His children, and
to enable us to live a holy life."

So, if we expect to gain the victory over sin and our bad habits,
we must follow God's Word. I have memorized a handful of Bible
promises and claim them, and then I thank God for the Holy Spirit
who supplies the power to overcome all inherited tendencies and
any environmental conditions I have lived with and now face. Let
me share with you more of my favorite statements made by Ellen
G. White and the Scriptures.

Our High Calling, page 131, says, "We need to educate the soul
to lay hold, and hold fast to the rich promises of Christ. The Lord
Jesus knows that it is not possible for us to resist the many temptations of Satan" in our fallen human nature. As the apostle Paul
says in Romans 7:1–25, our only hope is "as we shall have divine
power given us from God."

So, as Psalms 34:8 appeals, "O taste and see that the Lord is
good, blessed is the man that trusted in him." Now here are some
of my favorite Bible scriptures that can help us all.

A. "But thanks be to God, which giveth us the victory through
   our Lord Jesus Christ" (1 Corinthians 15:57).
B. "I can do all things through Christ which strengtheneth me"
   (Philippians 4:13).
C. "Great peace have they which love thy law: and nothing shall
   offend them" (Psalm 119:165).
D. "Where the Spirit of the Lord" is men's souls are set free (2
   Corinthians 3:17).
E. God's power works best "in weakness" (2 Corinthians 12:9).
F. He guides the humble in what is right and teaches them His
   way (Psalm 25:9).
G. "In all these things we are more than conquerors through him
   that loved us" (Romans 8:37).

In summary, I will leave you with a two-part help that I have used over and over again.

A. What to do? Ask God for help as soon as you sense Satan's attacks.
B. Claim His promises and stand on them. This has worked for me.

Chapter 7

A Prevention Plan

Friends, are you wondering why I am ending this book on the subject of prevention? The reason is very simple: prevention is worth a ton of cure—even if we have deeply fallen and became addicted to sex, smoking, drinking, gambling, or something else. A fact of note is that God *can* deliver you out of sin and bad habits, and He *does* deliver you out of sin and bad habits. If now, by your own choice, you have overcome sins, such as the lust of the flesh and of the eyes, and the pride of this world, your new life has just begun.

Therefore, let me share some tools and facts with you from over thirty years of teaching students in drug prevention education. My goal now is to help you live a daily life of victory in Jesus, which is reflected in the title of this book. Remember that we all are preparing for Jesus to come back, and soon He will take us to our heavenly home. That is why we need daily victory. Paul says, "Tribulation worketh patience" (Romans 5:3). The tribulation that we will all soon go through will be a time for character building day by day and night by night. So, it is our responsibility to hold onto Jesus, for He loves us too much to ever let us go. He promises, "I am with you alway, even unto the end of the world" (Matthew 28:20). His kingdom is coming soon!

Now, let me suggest some powerful reasons why prevention, since you have gotten the victory over x, y, and z, is so important. We daily walk in God's Spirit; we live like Him and for Him. So, to deal with the past, we must do as Paul described—"forgetting those things which are behind" (Philippians 3:13). If we had made different choices in the first place, we probably would not have these habits to overcome. So, please think along with me deeply now. What measures can we take to avoid falling back? I hope with all my heart that you give top billing to what I say next and implement the following steps.

1. I wish to give you "something better" than that which the world offers.
2. What God offers is to be our "higher power," as Alcoholics Anonymous describes.
3. Parents, God's Word has a lot to say about raising our children. In Daniel chapter 1, Daniel's early life education with his parents really paid off. At the age of about seventeen, he remained faithful to God. How was that possible? It was because good habits, formed early in life, remained with him, and the result was that he had clear thinking, wisdom, and understanding.
4. In verse 8, we read that he "purposed in his heart … not to defile himself with the portion of the king's meat" (probably unclean meats offered to idols) and to not defile himself "with the wine" that the king drank. Alcoholic wine, for a Jewish boy in God's service, was forbidden.

> **❝** *God gave me total victory—cold turkey—and, for the last thirty-eight years, my victory has remained.*

So, Daniel appealed to his master to give him ten days to prove himself on a diet of "pulse to eat, and water to drink" (Daniel 1:12). Thus, he was asking for what amounted to a vegetarian diet, if you will. Verse 15 tells us what the results were: "their countenances appeared fairer and fatter." They were healthier. Now, what happened next is truly God-given. Verse 17 tells us that God honored the young men who had been faithful to His Word with "all learning and wisdom."

At the end of their three years of university training, every student was to pass before the king in review. Verse 20 says that the results for Daniel and his companions were ten times better than for all the other students in his class. So, prevention really paid off, as it still does today. Satan's goal is to get our kids hooked as soon as possible, and he uses things such as:

1. Their peers,
2. Ads on social media,
3. The bad example of parents.

Satan knows that children get addicted very fast. Therefore, it behooves you, parents, to be on top of your children's life by example, example, and more example. Also, educate, educate, and further educate them to live a temperate life, drug and alcohol free, and centered on God.

Let me end with three life principles for prevention. I have found that prevention comes in three ways:

1. Daniel's parents taught Daniel solid values when he was young, and that is what my parents did for us, as my brother and I never saw Mom and Dad smoke, drink, or do drugs. Our home life was fun and full of love. We had a good diet, and we were taught Bible values. We also socialized with other Christian families. So, what went wrong? As I mentioned in chapter 1, when I was a young boy, I was put down when I failed in school, and I was ostracized by my classmates. This made me more open to another lifestyle. At age eighteen, I had begun smoking, and, at age nineteen, I was drinking. My actions were all in rebellion to what I had been taught.

2. As I became wilder and wilder, from ages seventeen to thirty-three, I now faced a great life crisis: divorce! It threw me for a loop. But I was not done with my non-Christian life just yet. While attending Chico State University, in California, I still smoked MJ and drank. So, now as I moved in with Mom and Dad to save money while going to college, the Holy Spirit began working on my heart. Mom's prayers were paying off as I met a Christian couple and saw something better in the way they lived their lives.

At this time, I made a choice to be temperate—no more alcohol, no more MJ. God gave me total victory—cold turkey—and, for the last thirty-eight years, my victory has remained. I was not addicted but was a social user on a recreational basis.

Now, how was I to stay clean?

A. A 100% new lifestyle.
B. A no drinking period.
C. Daily walking with God.
D. Becoming a Bible teacher at church.

So, as I studied God's Word and taught it, I became clean from my past sins. Now I developed a new set of habits, which were all designed to help me be blessed and to teach thousands of youths for twenty-eight years in drug prevention education in public and church schools. Each time I spoke to the teens, the principles solidified in my own mind such that I was never to fall backwards again.

3. So, prevention can come after being addicted and then being set free. As an example, my brother Norm has fallen off the wagon four times. He was addicted to alcohol, drugs, cigarettes, and MJ all at the same time. Most people would have written him off as a lost cause, but God did not and neither did I. Through much prayer, he received encouragement when he called me on the phone. More than one crisis befell him in his life. He ended up in the hospital, went through detox, and then returned home. He now sees the light and that he must make a 100% life change.

Norm struggles with temptation as the devil does not want to let him go. But facing major health problems, he is now wide awake. His goals became: changing his diet, which he has done; finding a good place to live; and again attending church. So, how did I help him out? By prayer and more prayer and, when we talked by phone, I always encouraged him and never put him down. I was basically there for him.

In conclusion, if I had to live life over again, I would make life choices as Daniel did from his teens to his adult life. He lived to be at least ninety years old. What a great Bible example he is for us to follow. So, now, at the age of seventy-four, as the scripture says, I am "redeeming the time" (Eph. 5:16).

This book is an attempt to help you live only for Jesus and be His disciple, as I choose to do on a daily basis. Now take a few minutes to fill in the last worksheet, "God's Plan of Prevention."

God's Plan of Prevention

1. Is prevention a relevant topic in today's world? Y __ N __
2. Where does prevention start? Home __ school __ or church __
3. Where does intemperance start?

_____

_____

4. What is a "gateway drug"?

_____

_____

Name some examples.

_____

5. We must daily choose to have Christ in our decision making. Y __ N __

6. The best solution for our youth is to offer something better than the world offers. Name some.

_____

_____

7. Does drunkenness start at the home kitchen table? Y __ N __

8. Name some current lifestyle practices in your home now that, after reading this presentation, make you see the need to change those practices.

_____

_____

9. Appetite is educated to crave something stronger. Can this lead to wrong lifestyle habits? Y __ N __

10. We should forget to teach about the laws of health to our children. Y __ N __

11. The only safe course in life is to touch not, taste not, and handle not tea, coffee, and wine. Y __ N __

12. Always reason from cause to effect. Y __ N __

13. Forget about teaching self-denial and self-control, for the youth will learn this by themselves. Y __ N __

14. Evil habits can be blocked by positive choices taught to the children by the parents and at a very early age. Y __ N __

15. In addition, you might consider, as a parent, to monitor your children and their associations. Make good choices with them, such as _____

_____

_____

14. Daniel knew what was best for him (because his parents had taught him at home), and he chose God's diet plan. How can we do likewise today with all the temptations coming at us?

_____

_____

15. List several steps in their proper order, using Daniel 1:8-21, demonstrating how Daniel used God's word with its health laws to honor God and preserve his God-given talents and gifts. Here is a start:
    a. He resolved (purposed) in his heart not to defile himself. (vs. 8).
    b. He made a decision, by refusing specific foods and drinks, to follow God's Word. (vs. 8).

A Final Word

D ear friends of mine, now you have read and studied my life story. As my dear friend Ron said in the foreword, I have laid out a map, a blueprint, for anyone to follow. As a dedicated Christian author of three books, overcoming my life issues has been a struggle at times. But, my dear friend, Jesus has provided His grace and His love to help me be where I am today step by step and day by day.

His promise, found in Revelation 12:11, states this so well: "And they overcame him by the blood of the Lamb, and by the word of their testimony; and they loved not their lives unto the death." Paraphrasing this verse, with commentary, I will insert my name, as you can insert yours:

1. And *Bruce* overcame Satan and his legions of angels.
2. How? "By the blood of the lamb." His victory on the cross is mine as I accept Him by faith as my personal Savior and Lord.
3. And what are the fruits? *Bruce* has given you "the word of" his "testimony." You can now tell others as well, and you will be very blessed if you do.
4. And last of all, *Bruce* is not afraid of dying for his faith. He declares: "It is a joy to suffer as my Lord did for me."

So, my life story went from the bottom, with attention-deficit/hyperactivity disorder (ADHD), as I failed at almost all that I did and finished high school with a C-minus. Next, I went to the United States Air Force for four-and-a-half years. And then I went on to a junior college in Los Angeles, California, where I almost bombed out with three D's the first year. But I was determined to go from a Z-plan in my life to an A-plan.

I spent as much time in the library as possible along with summer school, staying with it because I was determined to graduate college.

In four years plus the goal was met with a C+ grade point average. So, all the odds were against me. To this day, I have never learned phonics. So this presents me with a learning challenge daily. But I do have a good memory, and what I need to learn I must go over and over to let it sink in.

At the age of thirty-three, I started graduate school in California at Chico State. In two-and-one-half years, I finished the program with a "B" average—my best ever. From there, I went to post-seminary Bible training school in Chicago for a crash nine-month training period. Then I went to Pennsylvania.

It was in Pennsylvania that I started my life calling. My responsibility was to fund-raise from the business community and then lecture at both the junior and senior high school level to educate teens to see a better way than drugs and alcohol. This career, this calling, lasted twenty-eight years. During that time, I talked with thousands of business owners to fund the school program, and I talked to many thousands of teens. It is my goal to see many of these teens in God's kingdom soon.

Now at the age of seventy-four, my new life goal is to help you also to follow God's blueprint map as I share with you how my life of service has helped others and myself as well. I overcame through God's power and the Holy Spirit's presence in my life every day. I still need His power and blessing to help others. Daily prayer and Bible study is always on my agenda—morning, noon, and to end the day.

So, may God guide you all, and I hope to see you in heaven some day.

If you wish to contact me, feel free to email me by entering this link in your web browser: https://1ref.us/r9457092

References

1. Ellen G. White, *Steps to Christ*, published by Review and Herald Publishing Association.

2. Ellen G. White, *Our High Calling*.

3. Alcoholics Anonymous, Grand Central Station, New York, 10163. My A.A. card, data selected from.

TEACH Services, Inc.
P U B L I S H I N G

We invite you to view the complete
selection of titles we publish at:
www.TEACHServices.com

We encourage you to write us
with your thoughts about this,
or any other book we publish at:
info@TEACHServices.com

TEACH Services' titles may be purchased in
bulk quantities for educational, fund-raising,
business, or promotional use.
bulksales@TEACHServices.com

Finally, if you are interested in seeing
your own book in print, please contact us at:
publishing@TEACHServices.com
We are happy to review your manuscript at no charge.

CPSIA information can be obtained
at www.ICGtesting.com
Printed in the USA
LVHW051534030223
738545LV00007B/86